My GOD Moments

JEAN FOSTER

ISBN 979-8-88751-987-6 (paperback)
ISBN 979-8-88751-988-3 (digital)

Copyright © 2023 by Jean Foster

All rights reserved. No part of this publication may be reproduced, distributed, or transmitted in any form or by any means, including photocopying, recording, or other electronic or mechanical methods without the prior written permission of the publisher. For permission requests, solicit the publisher via the address below.

Christian Faith Publishing
832 Park Avenue
Meadville, PA 16335
www.christianfaithpublishing.com

Printed in the United States of America

Dedicated to my children: Suzette, Larry Jr., and Trina, whom I love so much. They are my inspiration and my best blessings from God.

CONTENTS

Chapter 1: A Son 1
Chapter 2: Surrender 4
Chapter 3: Day Care 9
Chapter 4: You Can't Have a Void 11
Chapter 5: Hold Me 15
Chapter 6: Forgive Martha 17
Chapter 7: Love-Balloon 20
Chapter 8: Mobile Home 22
Chapter 9: Car 24
Chapter 10: Promotion 26
Chapter 11: Suzette Smart 28
Chapter 12: Remove the Feathers 29
Chapter 13: The House I Got and the One I Didn't Get 31
Chapter 14: Hamels 34
Chapter 15: Mail the Books 35
Chapter 16: Estelle Prayer 37
Chapter 17: Seat Belts 39
Chapter 18: Wickette Healed 40
Chapter 19: Clothes 42
Chapter 20: Carolyn Needs Prayer 43
Chapter 21: 91st Psalm 45
Chapter 22: Keebler Healed 48
Chapter 23: Cancer Scare 49

Chapter 24: Josh 51
Chapter 25: Job—Ask for It..52
Chapter 26: Financial Blessing 53
Chapter 27: Job at Home..55
Chapter 28: New House and Job at Home..............................57
Chapter 29: Under the Cross 60
Chapter 30: Redeemed 61
Chapter 31: Child in Throne Room 63
Chapter 32: Crown..64
Chapter 33: Horse and Rider...66
Chapter 34: Lost Chick 69
Chapter 35: Adopted 70
Chapter 36: Jail..72
Chapter 37: Defective Human...74
Chapter 38: Birth-Death..75
Conclusion..77

Dear friends, I am longing to tell you of all the wonderful things that God has done. I know He loves you and will do the same kind of things for you. As I take you down the journey with God, I pray that you will learn to trust Him totally and obey Him completely. That's when you see His blessing. Of course, we will fail sometimes, but don't let that stop you. God always wants you to draw near to Him.

Discussion

Why should we repeat the things we have seen God do?

- In the Bible, people repeated the things God did to remind the next generation.
- It gives faith to those hearing it.
- It gives you a spirit of gratitude.
- Legacy for your children and grandchildren.

> Let them sacrifice thank offerings and tell of his works with songs of joy. (Psalm 107:22)

> They triumphed over him by the blood of the Lamb and by the word of their testimony; they did not love their lives so much as to shrink from death. (Revelation 12:11)

Many of the Samaritans from that town believed in him because of the woman's testimony, "He told me everything I ever did." (John 4:39)

Give praise to the LORD, proclaim his name; make known among the nations what he has done. (Psalm 105:1)

Each of you is to take up a stone on his shoulder, according to the number of the tribes of the Israelites, to serve as a sign among you. In the future, when your children ask you, "What do these stones mean?" tell them that the flow of the Jordan was cut off before the ark of the covenant of the LORD. When it crossed the Jordan, the waters of the Jordan were cut off. These stones are to be a memorial to the people of Israel forever. (Joshua 4:5–7)

CHAPTER 1

A Son

My first encounter with hearing His voice was…a son.

I grew up in church and always knew about God and Jesus. I walked the aisle at age ten, and I believe that I accepted what I knew about Jesus. That He died for my sins, and He would take me to heaven when I died. But sadly, I didn't grow in my understanding of God. I had the misconception that God was big and too busy to be bothered with my little problems. I should only ask Him for big important things—like when someone was dying or something.

I went on with my life; I married and had a daughter. I thought you would just plan your life, and it would happen that way. I had planned that I would have my second child two or three years apart from my first. We had a farm and wanted a boy to pass the farm down to. So I planned the date to go off the pill, and I just knew I would have the baby at the time I had planned. I was so excited to find that I was pregnant just as I had planned. But between the third and fourth months, I miscarried. When I went to the doctor, he told me that I had only one chance in a million to conceive and even then, I would not carry. My heart was breaking.

We went on and tried different medicines and things to get pregnant, but month after month I was disappointed. The months turned into a year, then two years and then three years. I had tried not to hope anymore. It was just too painful.

Then came my first direct encounter with God. Each night, I tucked my daughter in, and we said the prayer "Now I lay me down to sleep." By this time my daughter was five years old. She said, "Mommy, let's pray for me to have a little brother." My heart was racing. That's what I wanted most of all. But in my mind, I was thinking, *What if it doesn't happen? Then Suzette will be disappointed and maybe she wouldn't believe in God.* Then from deep inside me a voice said, "What about you? Do you believe?" My heart was about to pound out of my chest. I felt like I was standing on top of a fence, and I had to choose which way to go. I knew this was going to be a life-changing decision. Then I just made a leap and thought, *I'm going to believe.* Immediately, I felt an overpowering peace come over me, and I knew that it was done. We prayed for that baby brother together. That month I got pregnant, and nine months later, I had a healthy baby boy. That's how I learned to talk to God about things in my life. A little child taught me to have childlike faith.

Discussion

Why do we have to ask?
 So you will know when it's answered and be thankful and glorify God.
Does God always give you what you want?
 Good parents say yes sometimes and no sometimes and wait sometimes

Ask, Seek, Knock: **Ask** and it will be given to you; seek and you will find; knock and the door will be opened to you. (Matthew 7:7)

I keep **ask**ing that the **God** of our Lord Jesus Christ, the glorious Father, may give you the Spirit of wisdom and revelation so that you may know him better. (Ephesians 1:17)

If any of you lacks wisdom, you should **ask God**, who gives generously to all without finding fault, and it will be given to you. (James 1:5)

You desire but do not have, so you kill. You covet but you cannot get what you want, so you quarrel and fight. You do not have because you do not **ask God**. (James 4:2)

This is the confidence we have in approaching **God**: that if we **ask** anything according to his will, he hears us. (1 John 5:14)

CHAPTER 2

Surrender

As time went on, things took a turn for the worse. I now had three children. My marriage was falling apart. I was so distraught. I knew the Bible said that God didn't want a divorce. So I prayed and prayed for my husband to stop seeing other women and love me. I didn't pray this because I wanted God's will but because it was what I wanted. Things didn't get better.

Months passed. I tried to leave. I went to my parents' house and stayed for a couple of weeks. I cried the whole time. Finally, I came home with my tail between my legs. I tried to find a job. I filled out applications in every store in our small town. Time went by, but there were no replies. I was defeated. I cried all the time and didn't want to eat. I didn't dress myself or the children in the mornings. I was in such bad shape that my friends came over to talk to me. They said that if I didn't pull myself together, I would be put in a mental ward, and then what would happen to my children?

One night my friends said I needed to get out of the house, so they invited me to go night fishing with them. We were on the Mississippi River. That river is big and deep and has whirlpools that would suck a whole tree under. As I was looking over at the dark swirls, I thought I could just slide over the side of this boat, and I would be sucked under, and no one could rescue me. Then all this pain would be ended. My friend saw me move to the side of the boat.

She came and linked her arm to mine and made small talk. She never said she knew what I was thinking, but we both knew.

I think God looked down and said, "My child has had enough. I will send help to her." A few days later, a church called me and asked if I would interview for their part-time secretary position. They had gotten my application for the Ford Company, and I had checked that I would take a full-time, part-time, or temporary position. They couldn't find anyone who wanted a part-time position. I was overjoyed. I applied and got the job. This was the first ray of hope for the future.

As part of my job, I was to pick out clipped articles to use as fillers in the newsletter. One article said, "What do the children you teach see when they look at you?" I thought of my poor children seeing the basket case of a mother. I knew I needed help. Reading the Christian articles was some comfort to me. One day, I was at my grandmother's house, and I picked up the little book on a table beside her chair. The day's reading was titled, "I'm God's child. He loves me. And I'm important." It was different because it was written in the first person. The words were like water in a desert. I read them over and over again. I hadn't felt loved in so long. They spoke to my soul.

I ordered the monthly books for myself and began to read them daily. One night, I was reading at the kitchen table. The kids were in bed, and the house was quiet. The reading was about why God doesn't answer all prayers. It explained that it wasn't possible for God to answer some prayers. What if two teams were both praying to win the game between them? Many things we pray for involve changing another person.

God gave us free will. This free will is so treasured that He will not override it, even if it means that they reject Him and are lost forever. I was shocked. This means that I can't pray for God to make my husband change. I had nothing left to pray for. I surrendered. I prayed, "God, I give you everything, my marriage, my children, my life. Just make me right with you." And I meant it with all my heart. At that moment, I felt like I was lifted up into the heavenlies. I was wrapped in a warm blanket of love and power was running up and down me like electricity. I knew at that moment that I was going to be alright. A few days later, my friend said, "You are different, what changed?" I said, "God has changed me, and I don't know what my future holds, but I know that I'll be alright." I didn't get my husband to love me, but I found the greatest love ever.

Discussion

1. My first mistake was to put my husband over God. I thought he knew everything. I would like what he liked, do what he wanted, and so on. I had lost myself in the process.

   > And God spoke all these words: "I am the LORD your God, who brought you out of Egypt, out of the land of slavery. You shall have no other gods before me." (Exodus 20)

   Have you ever put something before God? A spouse, children, job, house, car, hobby?
   If you are struggling to surrender all, just ask God to help you.

2. I was so self-absorbed and caught up in my pain. I never realized what my wanting to kill myself would have done to my kids. It was years later that the impact of it hit me.

   Is something we're doing hurting someone else? Ask God to show you.

3. God will send help.

   > No temptation has overtaken you except what is common to mankind. And God is faithful; he will not let you be tempted beyond what you can bear. But when you are tempted, he will also provide a **way out** so that you can endure it. (1 Corinthians 10:13)

Have you ever been given a way out?

> Keep **you**r lives free from the love of money and be content with what **you** have, because God has said, "**Never** will I **leave you**; **never** will I forsake **you**." (Hebrews 13:5)

4. I'm God's child, He loves me, and I'm important.

   Important doesn't mean I'm better than anyone else; it means I'm important to God.
   Holy Spirit makes this truth abide in our hearts.
   Close your eyes and repeat the words, "I'm God's child, He loves me, and I'm important."

   > Then you **will** know the truth, and the truth **will** set you **free**. (John 8:32)

5. God won't override someone's free will. God will reach out to someone to draw them close to Him, but He will not force them.

   Have you ever prayed that God change someone else?
   Or have you prayed that God would change you and you noticed He did?
   Have you ever had a prayer not answered?
   Give an example of when He didn't, and you can look back and see that it was for your own good.

6. Full surrender is the place of total peace and love. This is where you meet God and see His miracles.

   > Then that person can pray to God and find favor with him, they **will** see God's face and

shout for joy; he **will** restore them to full well-being. (Job 33:26)

Would you like to fully surrender to God? You can pray for the grace to do it.

CHAPTER 3

Day Care

A couple of years passed. While I had peace on the inside, the situation was not any better. I was really tired of the emotional roller coaster. One day, I prayed, "God, either make this marriage right, and I will do whatever it takes on my part, or if it's never going to get better, then please make it over." My husband had moved to our tenant's house next door and was dating. The next day, he came in crying and said, "I don't know why I'm telling you this, but I'm not coming back." I had my answer. I packed our things, and I and the children left. I moved in with my parents.

I didn't know what to do next. I knew I would have to get a job and a day care, but I was scared to leave my children in day care. The headlines on the news that week were about abuse in day care, and they had never been left in day care before. The next Sunday, I went to a nearby church. I had been holding in all my tears so I wouldn't upset my children.

When I sat down in church, I relaxed, and all the tears began to flow. I went into the foyer to try to get a grip. An usher asked me if I needed help. I said that I didn't, but he was wise and got two women to talk to me. They took me to a back room, and I spilled out all my feeling. How I was so hurt about the separation and how I needed a job. Also how I had never left my children, and I was afraid of leaving them in day care. The first lady was so kind and compassionate. She explained that she had lost a child, and she knew what that pain was like. She reassured me that it would get better in time. The next lady spoke up and said, "I don't know why I am here because I don't think I have any wisdom to offer. I do work for the most sought-after day care in town. There's a yearlong waiting list to get in. I'm going to talk to my boss and see if we can help you." As it turned out, her boss did accept my three children in their day care, and she also said that since I was in a bad situation financially, she would let my children attend for free, and I could make the first payment when I got my first paycheck.

Discussion

1. The church is a place to praise God, learn about God, and get strength in times of trouble.

    > Not forsaking the **assembling** of ourselves together, as *is* the manner of some, but exhorting *one another*, and so much the more as you see the Day approaching. (Hebrews 10:25)

2. The people in the church are mostly kind and helpful and try to please God. This is a place to help one another. (Of course, as in any group, there are a few exceptions.)
    We should forgive each other's faults and bond together in love.

3. What did you see that God had to line up to make this happen? Right location. Right people. Wisdom of the usher.

    > God's voice thunders in marvelous **ways**; he does great things beyond our understanding. (Job 37:5)

CHAPTER 4

You Can't Have a Void

After the separation, I would lie in bed and think about my ex. I would picture him in bed with his new girlfriend. My stomach would churn, and I'd lay awake for hours. I was so unhappy and tired. I would try to blank out my mind so I could sleep, but it wouldn't work. I prayed, "God, help me stop thinking about this." I felt Him say, "You can't have a void. You have to fill it with something else." So I quoted the few scriptures that I knew in my mind. Then I would sing in my mind the Christian songs that I knew. I would end up with, "Jesus loves me" over and over. It was working. As long as I had Christian things going in my mind, the bad painful thoughts were not there. I would finally fall peacefully asleep. After three nights like this, I could go to sleep right away.

Discussion

1. Even though I was set free from hopeless despair by a touch from God, I still had to go through the grieving process. But I was never hopeless again.
2. Have you struggled with painful thoughts? Name some painful thoughts. (Hurt, anger, fear, lust, greed, self-doubt, etc.)
    Where do they come from? Satan is always trying to tear us down.

3. Find a scripture that fits your problem and memorize it. Tell the scripture to Satan every time the painful thoughts come. He will flee.
   Tell us about your painful thoughts and did scripture help?
   Find your special verse at www.biblegateway.com.

   Casting down imaginations, and every high thing that exalts itself against the knowledge of God, and bringing into captivity every thought to the obedience of Christ. (2 Corinthians 10:5)

   Submit yourselves therefore to God. Resist the **devil**, and he **will flee** from you. (James 4:7)

   When an impure spirit comes out of a person, it goes through arid places seeking rest and does not find it. Then it says, "I will return to the house I left." When it arrives, it finds the house swept clean and put in order. Then it goes and takes seven other spirits more wicked than itself, and they go in and live there. And the final condition of that person is worse than the first. (Luke 11:24–26)

   But thou art holy, O thou that inhabits the **praise**s of his people. (When God is present, Satan flees.) (Psalm 22:3)

   But he was wounded for **our** transgressions, he was bruised for **our** iniquities: the **chastisement of our peace** was upon him; and with his stripes we are healed. (Isaiah 53:5)

What does *chastisement* of our peace mean? (According to the dictionary, it means severe criticism; a rebuke or strong reprimand; corporal punishment; a beating.) (me—disturb)

Jesus takes away what disturbs our peace.

Hurt

> The LORD is near to them that are of a broken heart; and saves such that has a contrite(crushed) spirit. (Psalm 34:18)

Anger

> Be ye angry, and sin not: let not the sun go down upon your wrath. (Ephesians 4:26)

> Dearly beloved, avenge not yourselves, but rather give place unto wrath: for it **is** written, **Vengeance is mine**; I will repay, saith the Lord. (Romans 12:19)

Don't feel like no one will fight for you. God will repay. I just say, "That's not my problem. It's God's."

Lust

> Flee also youthful **lust**s: but follow righteousness, faith, charity, peace, with them that call on the Lord out of a pure heart. (2 Timothy 2:22)

Self-doubt

> Being **confident** of this very thing, that he which hath begun a good work in you will per-

form it until the day of Jesus Christ: you are a good work. (Philippians 1:6)

Fear

So do not fear, for I am with you; do not be dismayed, for I am your God. I will strengthen you and help you; I will uphold you with my righteous right hand. (Isaiah 41:10)

The **weapon**s we fight with are not the **weapon**s of the world. On the contrary, they have divine power to demolish strongholds. (2 Corinthians 10:4)

Worry

Therefore I tell you, do not worry about your life, what you will eat or drink; or about your body, what you will wear. Is not life more than food, and the body more than clothes? Look at the birds of the air; they do not sow or reap or store away in barns, and yet your heavenly Father feeds them. Are you not much more valuable than they? (Matthew 6:25–26)

Finally, brethren, whatsoever things are true, whatsoever things are honest, whatsoever things are just, whatsoever things are pure, whatsoever things are lovely, whatsoever things are of good report; if there be any virtue, and if there be any praise, think on these things. (Philippians 4:8)

CHAPTER 5

Hold Me

When I was going through a divorce, I would lay in bed and ask God: Why didn't my husband love me? Did I do something wrong? Is there something that would make me more interesting and fun? But I never heard an answer. You see, I wanted an answer so I could be in control next time. Finally, one night, I said, "I'm tired of trying to figure this out. God, just hold me." At that moment the room was filled with love. I could feel God holding me. I drifted off to sleep in perfect peace.

Discussion

1. Have you ever tried to change the unique special person that God made you to be, just to try to please someone else? Did it work?
2. If you need to change, God will show you. Otherwise, don't worry about it.
3. Tell us about a time you didn't get what you prayed for.
4. Did you get an explanation from God?
5. Did you later understand why you didn't get what your prayer for?
6. What if you never understand? Learn to trust God.

7. Is it wrong to ask God for a reason? No, you can have an honest conversation with God, but if you don't get an answer, learn to let it go and ask God to heal you of it.
8. Can you think of someone who didn't get what they prayed for in the Bible? Jesus in the garden.

> But let all those that put their **trust** in you rejoice: let them ever shout for joy, because you defend them: let them also that love your name be joyful in you. (Psalm 5:11)

> But I have **trust**ed in thy mercy; my heart shall rejoice in thy salvation. (Psalm 13:5)

> Show your marvelous lovingkindness, O thou that saves by thy right hand them which put their **trust** in thee from those that rise up against them. (Psalm 17:7)

> The Lord is my rock, and my fortress, and my deliverer; my God, my strength, in whom I will **trust**; my buckler, and the horn of my salvation, and my high tower. (Psalm 18:2)

> Trust in the Lord with all your heart and **lean not** on your own understanding; in all your ways submit to him, and he will make your paths straight. (Proverbs 3:5–6)

> He says, "**Be still, and know that I am God**; I will **be** exalted **am**ong the nations, I will **be** exalted **in** the earth." (Psalm 46:10)

CHAPTER 6

Forgive Martha

After asking God to hold me each night for several weeks, I felt God say, "It's time to forgive Martha." She was the girlfriend living in my house. I wasn't about to forgive her. She should be crawling to me, begging my forgiveness. Didn't she even have any respect for marriage? The minute I thought this, God's presence left, and the room felt cold and lonely. The next night the same thing. "God hold me."

"Forgive Martha."

"No."

The room went cold. The third night. "God hold me."

"Forgive Martha." Then I said, "Please don't leave me. I don't know how I can forgive Martha, but I'm willing to try if you'll help me." Then I felt peace.

The next day, my friend called me. She started talking about Martha, even thought I had told her to never mention that name to me. She told me that Martha had a bad childhood and that she had married very young. Her husband was abusive. Now she was living with my husband but was so jealous of everyone. She was a nervous wreck every time he left the house, especially when he came to my house to get the children. She was living in the hell that I had been living in. She had been looking for love everywhere, and she didn't even have Jesus. Suddenly, my heart went out to her, and I was able to forgive her. I started healing quicker now. God gave me baby steps to help me forgive.

Discussion

1. Do you think that forgiving others and getting forgiven ourselves go hand in hand?
2. Have you ever tried to have a conversation with someone who has unforgiveness and bitterness? Is it pleasant? Give examples.
3. Does having our minds filled with unforgiveness keep us from enjoying life? Give examples.
4. Does having our minds filled with unforgiveness block us from hearing from God? Tell us how it was if you ever experienced this.
5. Is it painful to be filled with unforgiveness? Give us an example.
6. Was God doing this for Martha's sake, my sake, or God's sake? Explain why. Martha didn't know or care. I needed to be free of the pain. God wanted to talk to me, but unforgiveness was in the way.
7. Is there a connection between being forgiven and getting healed? Give some examples. Unforgiveness affects your insides—blood pressure, ulcers, heart attacks, headaches, etc.

    (Not all sickness is due to unforgiveness so don't judge others.)
8. Quote: "But Jesus, I don't want to forgive them. They are **wrong**." Jesus answers, "Of course they are wrong. You don't have to forgive people who are right."
9. Unforgiveness and bitterness can be passed down to your children and **ruin** their lives.
10. Do you find forgiving someone very hard? Give an example.
11. Do you think that if it's too hard, you can ask God to help you with it?

> But if you do not **forgive** others their sins, your Father will not **forgive** your sins. (Matthew 6:15)

If my people, who are called by my name, will humble themselves and pray and seek my face and turn from their wicked ways, then I will hear from heaven, and I will **forgive** their sin and will **heal** their land. (2 Chronicles 7:14)

who **forgive**s all your sins and **heals** all your diseases. (Psalm 103:3)

And **forgive** us our debts, as we also have **forgive**n our debtors. (Matthew 6:12)

But if you do not **forgive** others their sins, your Father will not **forgive** your sins. (Matthew 6:15)

"And when you stand praying, if you hold anything against anyone, **forgive** them, so that your Father in heaven may **forgive** you your sins." (Mark 11:25)

If we confess our sins, he is faithful and just and will **forgive** us our sins and purify us from all unrighteousness. (1 John 1:9)

CHAPTER 7

Love-Balloon

I was asking God to hold me every night, and it was wonderful. One day I was so loving God's presence that I asked God to fill me with ALL His love. I immediately felt like a balloon being filled. With each pump, I was getting bigger and bigger. I cried out, "Stop! I'm going to burst!" Now I know that God loves us more than we can imagine. Never doubt that God loves you.

Discussion

The whole Bible tells of God's great love for you. I wish I could make you feel what I felt. Ask God to let you feel His love.

Tell of a time that you felt God's love so strong. Maybe during praise time at church. Or looking at a beautiful sunset, or flowers, or water, or stars, etc. Maybe as you drift off to sleep.

> Give thanks to the LORD, for he is good; his **love** endures forever. (Psalm 107:1)

> How priceless is your unfailing **love**, O **God**! People take refuge in the shadow **of** your wings. (Psalm 36:7)

Give thanks to the **God of** heaven. *His **love** endures forever.* (Psalm 136:26)

neither height nor depth, nor anything else in all creation, will be able to separate us from the **love of God** that is in Christ Jesus our Lord. (Romans 8:39)

For God so loved the world that he gave his one and only Son, that whoever believes in him shall not perish but have eternal life. (John 3:16)

CHAPTER 8

Mobile Home

I had found a job and had my children in day care, but I needed a place to live. I was living with my parents, but they didn't really have room. I and two of my children were sleeping on the hide-a-bed in the living room with the third child on a day bed. I remember being woke up in the night with my sister trying to convince her boyfriend to come on in; she was telling him that it was okay that we were on the hide-a-bed. Also I had no privacy to deal with all my emotions. And I also was concerned that it was not good for my children to be living with their grandparents full-time. When I said no food before dinner, they would say, "Well, Memaw will just give it to me." So I started looking for a place for four people. The apartments were expensive, and they wanted to check my credit. I had not established credit yet. I didn't know what to do.

That night, I asked God what I should do. I felt like He was saying to go visit my friend in the country. I didn't see where that would get me a place to live, but I thought maybe it was just to give me and my parents a break. So I visited Ann for the weekend. I was telling her my dilemma about a place to live. She said, "You should talk to Paul. He is selling his mobile home in town and moving back to the country." When I got back home, I called Paul and asked about the mobile home. He said, "There's only one person that I have told about selling my mobile home. You must have talked to Ann." The mobile home was just what I needed, a three-bedroom in a good school district. We went to the bank to see about my buying it. But I still had no credit. Paul said he would leave the note in his name, and I would take over the payments. The bank put a note in the file that when it was paid off, I would get the title.

CHAPTER 9

Car

My old car was starting to need a lot of repairs, and it got terrible gas mileage. I knew I needed a newer car. I still had no credit, and even the small cars were out of my price range. I prayed that night and asked God, "How am I going to get a car?" I felt He was saying go to my credit union. My company had just started a credit union a few months before. They explained that they would start by getting us the best interest rate they could get us. After three or four years, they would have enough money in the pot to start making loans. I thought what good would going to my credit union do. I thought maybe I was just checking my credit, or maybe I could establish some credit.

I went to Kathy's office and told her I was needing a car. She said, "Okay, what car are you looking at?" I told her that I didn't have a car in mind. She said, "I don't know how to look it up. I have to start with the make and model to see what your payments would be." I wondered why I was there. Then she said, "You should buy Tom's Thunderbird. It's brand-new and has leather seats and quad sound."

My friend had just bought a new Thunderbird, and I remember thinking that if I could have any car I wanted, it would be a Thunderbird. I told Kathy that a Thunderbird was way out of my price range. She said, "No, it's not. He is asking half the price for it. He bought it from his brother-in-law at cost and put a large payment down on it. When he brought it home, his wife was mad because she wanted a different car. Now he just wants someone to take it off his hands for what is owed on it." I couldn't believe it. I said, "Wow, how many people are fighting over this deal?" Kathy said, "None, I knew he wanted to sell it, but he just called me and gave me the price. You are the only one who knows it. Also I just got notice that we could start making car loans. You will be our first loan."

Discussion for chapters 8 and 9 (home and car)

1. Tell of a time that God told you to do something that didn't make sense.
2. Were you obedient?
3. What were the results?

> "For my thoughts are not your thoughts, neither are your ways my ways," declares the LORD. "As the heavens are higher than the earth, so are my ways higher than your ways and my thoughts than your thoughts." (Isaiah 55:8–9)

> If they **obey** and serve him, they will spend the rest of their days in prosperity and their years in contentment. (Job 36:11)

> Jesus replied, "Anyone who loves me will **obey** my teaching. My Father will love them, and we will come to them and make our home with them." (John 14:23)

> But Samuel replied: "Does the LORD delight in burnt offerings and **sacrifice**s as much as in obeying the LORD? To obey is **better than sacrifice**, and to heed is **better than** the fat of rams." (1 Samuel 15:22)

CHAPTER 10

Promotion

I had been working at a small job, typing address labels, and taking a course at college at night. When I finished my first course in accounting, my little job ended, and the company closed. With my new training, I was able to find a job in a few days working as an accounting clerk. When I had been there nine months, my supervisor decided to move and recommended I take her place. So I was promoted to supervisor of accounting clerks. After a year, we were having problems with communications between the land department and the accounting department. Our biggest customer threatened to leave us if we couldn't get their statements right. So they decided to form a new department, and a man for the land department would head it. He didn't want this job and wanted to get back to the land department. They promised him that once he got things organized and running smoothly, they would hire someone from the outside to be the manager of this department. I showed him the accounting side, and he trained me in the land side. By the time the year was coming to an end, he recommended me for the job of manager. I was promoted to manager.

The company had a profit-sharing policy. A percent of the year's profits was distributed based on job position and rating from your supervisor. That year was a record year in profits, and I had a high job position and a high rating. My bonus was enough for me to put a down payment on a house.

I worked for a few more years. But in time the work increased, and I found myself having to work late every night. I felt that my children needed me at home, and I should look for another job. One night, I was praying, and I told God that I just couldn't find the strength to leave. I liked the prestige too much. I asked Him to help me do the right thing. A few days later, I received a memo in my inbox saying that they were going to send the work done in my department to the various field offices and then dissolve my department. I would be kept on helping train the people, and then they would find a spot for me. I knew that God helped me do what I needed to do.

When I was telling this story to a friend, my daughter commented, "Wow, God formed a department for you when you came and dissolved it when you left."

Discussion

1. Do you see the timing it took to make all this work?
2. Have you ever looked back and saw the plan God had for you?
3. Tell us about it.

> "For I know the plans I have for you," declares the Lord, "plans to prosper you **and** not to harm you, plans to give you **hope and a future**." (Jeremiah 29:11)

CHAPTER 11

Suzette Smart

When Suzette was in upper elementary school, I was contacted to let me know that she was tested and would be put in the gifted-talented class. I remembered back when she was about three years old. I was sitting on the couch reading the small local paper. My friend's daughter made the A-B honor roll. I looked out the window and saw Suzette swinging on the swing set. It was more of a wish than a prayer. I thought, *O God, I wish Suzette would be smart.* Now years later I realized that God had answered this wish. She went on to be valedictorian of her class and graduated from college magna cum laude.

Discussion

This wish was fulfilled even before I learned to pray specifically. Maybe God granted it at that moment or maybe later.

Tell us about a time you saw later when God had been working in your life, and you didn't know it.

Did you get more than you asked? Give examples.

Take delight in the LORD, and he will give you the **desires of your heart**. (Psalm 37:4)

CHAPTER 12

Remove the Feathers

I was living in a nice mobile home in a nice park. We were very happy there for four years, but I had my young son and daughter in the same bedroom with bunk beds. I knew that as they got older, they would need their own bedrooms. Also it was too far for my children to walk to their after-school activities, so they couldn't participate. I didn't know what I was going to do, as I could not afford a house.

Things suddenly became uncomfortable in the park. The owner started accusing my children of stealing mail when they were not even in town. Then he called me to say that my dog was running loose, but he was laying at my feet. He would even stop my guest coming into the park and say that they were speeding. I couldn't understand why everything was going wrong when we had been happy there. Then one day I heard a preacher on TV saying that when it was time for the baby birds to leave the nest, the mother bird would remove the soft warm feathers lining the nest, leaving the sticks to prick them. That is sometimes God's way of moving us to the next step.

I thought that must be what was happening to me. So I started looking into moving the mobile home to my own land. But to buy land you had to put down 20 percent and then you had to build a driveway, a sewer system, and electrical and gas connections, and then there was the cost of moving the home. It was way more than the down payment on a house. I started looking for a house that had room for us and was close enough to school so my children could participate in extracurricular activities. I had a nice Christmas bonus that year and was able to get everything we needed. More than I thought we could. I just needed a push.

Discussion

1. I was hung up by wrong thinking. I thought I could never afford a house. It wasn't sinful thinking, but it was blocking me from having the blessing God wanted me to have. God had to give me a push.
    Give examples of some wrong thinking that blocks God's best. (Can't afford it. Too hard for me. Protect myself from hurt.)
2. What can you do about it? (Ask God to show you if you have any wrong thinking.)
3. Can bad times turn out to be a blessing?

> The **blessing** if you obey the commands of the LORD your God that I am giving you today. (Deuteronomy 11:27)

> Trust in the LORD with all your heart and **lean no**t on your own understanding. (Proverbs 3:5)

> My mouth will tell of your righteous deeds, of your saving acts all day long—though I **know not** how to relate them all. (Psalm 71:15)

CHAPTER 13

The House I Got and the One I Didn't Get

It was time to get a new house. We were needing another bedroom to separate my son and daughter from the same room. Also the children were missing out on after-school activities because it was too far for them to walk, and I was not home to take them. I went to a realtor and told her I needed a four-bedroom house near the school, and it could not be over a certain dollar amount per month. She said, "You are wanting a miracle." I said, "Yes, that's what I need." After a few months, she found a house that fit my requests.

Someone wanted a large down payment and take over a small monthly note. She was able to talk them into owner financing the large down payment. The house was so great. I would drive by it every day and dream how wonderful it would be. The problem was that I was going to use the Christmas bonus that I expected to receive to make the down payment on the house. It was November, and I would not get my bonus for a month. A friend offered to loan me the money, but I didn't think that would be right. I said, "If it's meant to be, the house will be there when I have my money." Well, the house sold a week before I got my money. I was very disappointed.

Soon after that, I was telling a friend at church that I needed a four-bedroom house within walking distance of the school my children attended. She said she had some friends that had a house with three bedrooms and a private living room that could be used as a bedroom. They had it on the market, and it didn't sell. They had given up and taken it off the market. I looked at it and knew it would meet my needs. But I was a little sad that it wasn't as nice as the first house. We moved into the house and were very happy there.

I had to drive past the first house every day to go to work. I always wondered why I didn't get the first house which was much nicer. One night I was coming home late, and I saw a gang of teenagers in the yard of the first house. I told my neighbor that it was odd to see all those kids in the yard so late at night. She said, "Don't you know that that is the place the drug deals are done because it backs up to a quick-service store." I was so glad that I didn't get the first house. My kids would have been home alone in the afternoons subject to that influence. Now I know why God didn't give me the first house. He was protecting my children.

Discussion

1. Have you ever wanted something and then later were glad you didn't get it?
2. Do you think God knows the hidden things about what we are trying to do or get?

> But let all who take refuge in you be glad; let them ever sing for joy. Spread your **protect**ion over them, that those who love your name may rejoice in you. (Psalm 5:11)

> You, LORD, will keep the needy safe and will **protect** us forever from the wicked. (Psalm 12:7)

> You are my hiding place; you will **protect** me from trouble and surround me with songs of deliverance. (Psalm 32:7)

"Because he loves me," says the Lord, "I will rescue him; I will **protect** him, for he acknowledges my name." (Psalm 91:14)

CHAPTER 14

Hamels

My children had been saving their allowance to go to Hamel's Park and ride the rides. Their allowance was only about $1 a week, so it took a long time, but they had saved $5 each. They were so excited. We had been there a short time before Larry came to me crying. He had lost his money. We looked around the park and even in the car but couldn't find it. I had no money to replace it. I was so sad for him. I asked God to help us find the money. I felt that God was saying, "Tell him to go watch the rides." He walked back dejectedly. A few minutes he came back overjoyed. He had found a five-dollar bill. But he had lost five ones.

Discussion

Tell us about a time you lost something, and God restored it with something else.

> Then the LORD your God will **restore** your fortunes and have compassion on you and gather you again from all the nations where he scattered you. (Deuteronomy 30:3)

> **Restore** us, God Almighty; make your face shine on us, that we may be saved. (Psalm 80:7)

CHAPTER 15

Mail the Books

This shows the importance of not getting distracted. I was single and wished to meet Mr. Right. My neighbor wanted me to meet her brother. She showed me his picture, and he was very handsome. I went to bed each night, asking God if this man could be the right one. I never got an answer. After a few nights, I changed my prayer to, "What do you want me to do?" Immediately I felt that God was saying to mail three certain books to Bobbie. I knew Bobbie from the church that I would attend with my cousin when I visited her. They said that Bobbie's husband had left her, and she was so distressed. I knew what that pain felt like, and my heart went out to her. So I got up and picked out the three books for Bobbie. I laid them on the table so I would remember to mail them tomorrow.

When I got back in bed, I felt that God was saying to get them wrapped. So I got up and wrapped them for mail. I went back to bed, and again I felt that God wanted me to look up the address and put stamps on them, so they were totally ready for the next day. Finally, I could rest. I mailed them the next day. After a few weeks, I was visiting my cousin again. I saw Bobbie at church. She ran to me and hugged me and said, "Those books saved my life. I was so depressed that I didn't want to live. When those books came, I stayed up all night and read all three of them. They gave me the will to live." I thought, *And I almost missed God's voice being so wrapped up in what I wanted.*

Discussion

1. Tell us about a time you were so self-absorbed, you almost missed helping someone.
2. If you are not getting an answer from God, change your prayer.
3. Tell us about a time you were so self-absorbed, you almost missed some blessing God had for you.

> But Martha was **distract**ed by all the preparations that had to be made. She came to him and asked, "Lord, don't you care that my sister has left me to do the work by myself? Tell her to help me!"
>
> "Martha, Martha," the Lord answered, "you are worried and upset about many things, but few things are needed—or indeed only one. Mary has chosen what is better, and it will not be taken away from her." (Luke 10:40–42)

Would you like to sit a Jesus's feet and ask questions? What wonderful things might Jesus be telling Mary? Wouldn't you hate to miss this opportunity?

CHAPTER 16

Estelle Prayer

My friend, Estelle, had a little boy, but he only lived two days. She was so devastated that she would not try to have another baby for ten years. Finally, she felt she was ready to try again, and she stopped taking the pill. She started having terrible pains in her stomach. The doctor said her tubes were blocked, and they would have to clean them out. When they tried to do the procedure, the doctor told her that it didn't work. That she had repeated infections, and her tubes were solid scar tissue all the way up, and there was no way she would have another child. Estelle called me crying. She was so heartbroken. I said we could pray. She's Catholic and uses a prayer book. She said that there wasn't a prayer in her book that fit the situation. I said, "Let's just pray from our hearts." We prayed and decided that if God wanted her to have another child, He would make the impossible happen. A few months later, she went to the doctor and found out that she was pregnant. The doctor said he didn't see how that could have possibly happened, but we know it was God.

Discussion

Since God gave me a baby when I was told it was impossible, it was easy to have faith that God could do it for Estelle. Tell of a time God did something for you that you could use to help someone else.

> The Lord remembered her. So in the course of time, Hannah became pregnant and gave birth to a son. She named him Samuel, saying, "Because I asked the Lord for him." (1 Samuel 1:20)

CHAPTER 17

Seat Belts

I was driving an old two-door car, and the seat belts were cut out of it. I had planned to get a newer car with seat belts. Before I could come up with the money for a new car, I was stopped and given a ticket for no seat belts. I was mad. I said, "God, it's not my fault that I couldn't afford a new car." I felt God say, "Thank me for the ticket." Well, that was not easy to do, but I grudgingly said, "Thank you for the ticket, and I want to really mean it." A week later, a car ran a red light and hit my daughter and spun her car around. She was not hurt because she was wearing her seat belt. She told me that the only reason she had been wearing her seat belt was because I had gotten that ticket.

Discussion

Tell us of a time that something that seemed evil turned out to be good.

> But as **for** you, ye thought **evil** against me; but God **meant** it unto good, to bring to pass, as it is this day, to save much people alive. (Genesis 50:20)

CHAPTER 18

Wickette Healed

I was riding in the car with my friend, and I was petting her dog in the back seat. I said, "Whatever happened to that mean dog you had? He would growl at you with his hair standing on end." She said, "That's him that you are petting." I was shocked and snatched my hand back. "I can't believe it. What did you do to change him?" I said. "We prayed for him," she said. I didn't know you could pray for animals.

When I got home, I looked at my dog. His eyes were starting to get that milky blue that makes them lose their eyesight. So I just casually put my hand on his head and said, "Be healed in the name of Jesus." I did that every day for a week but didn't give it much thought. A few weeks later, I was very distressed because I had run out of the dog's seizure medicine. And it was the weekend, and I couldn't get more until Monday. Every time we missed a day of medicine, he would have terrible seizures. One day passed and no seizures. I refilled the medicine but didn't give it to him. After a week and then a month, he had not had a seizure, and I realized that he had indeed been healed by Jesus. He lived five more years and never had another seizure.

Discussion

God cares about small things, even animals. Tell us of a small thing that God answered your prayer.

> Are not two **sparrow**s sold for a farthing? And one of them shall not fall on the ground without your Father. (Matthew 10:29)

CHAPTER 19

Clothes

Being single with three children, I didn't have enough money to buy myself nice clothes. But people would give me the most beautiful clothes; some were silk and wool. Even when I changed jobs, new people would give me clothes. I considered this God blessing me. One day Linda called me. She said, "When you told me that God gave you clothes, I didn't believe you. No one had ever given me clothes. Today, I was at work, and I took the trash out of the back alley. When I returned to my desk, I felt God was telling me to go back to the alley. I thought, *Why? I was just there, and there was nothing there.* But I kept feeling that I should go. When I went to the alley, I found a huge box full of nice clothes, and half were my size, and half are your size."

Discussion

When you tell of God's blessings, it gives God a chance to prove Himself to others. Tell of a time you encouraged someone by telling of what God has done for you.

> Consider the lilies how they grow: they toil not, they spin not; and yet I say unto you, that Solomon in all his glory was not arrayed like one of these. (Luke 12:27)

CHAPTER 20

Carolyn Needs Prayer

We met every Friday at noon for Bible study and prayer. At the end, we formed a circle and joined our hands for prayer. That particular Friday, I felt that someone had an urgent prayer need. I went around the circle in my mind. Does this one need prayer? After a few people, I looked at Carolyn and asked in my mind. Is this the one that needs prayer? An overwhelming feeling came over me. I wanted to hold her and comfort her like a hurt child and say, "It's alright." I went around the circle twice to be sure, and I had the same feeling when I came to Carolyn. So I said, "Carolyn, why don't you stand in the middle? I feel like you need special prayer." She said, "Oh, thank you. I had a bad dream last night that my son, Jamie, died. I didn't want to confess negative things, but I couldn't break the bad feeling all day." So we prayed for her.

That Sunday night while everyone was at church, there came a call. Her son, Jamie, and the pastor's son were in a terrible accident on their way back to college. Their car had run under an eighteen-wheeler that was turning and was across the road sideways. The top of the car was decapitated. When the sheriff arrived, he got the name from the license plate, but the ambulance had already left. There were two hospitals the same distance away, but in different directions, and they didn't know which hospital they were taken to. They said they would let us know more as soon as they had a word. For two hours the church members stayed and prayed as the parents were in fear and distress. Finally, the word came and both young men were okay. God was wanting to comfort Carolyn and tell her it was okay.

Discussion

You can see God's heart, wanting to comfort us.

> Surely he has borne our griefs and carried our sorrows. (Isaiah 53:4)

A few weeks later, at the Friday prayer, I had the same feeling that someone needed special prayer. I went to each person in my mind and asked, "Is it this one?" When it came to me, the feeling was strong that it was me. I went around again to be sure. I was very troubled. Was one of my children in trouble?

After the meeting, I left the building quickly, I felt that I needed to pray and understand what was wrong. Carolyn said, "I'll walk out with you." I was too distracted to pay her much attention. When we came to the corner where we would part ways, she said, "I'll walk all the way to your office." When we were there, she hugged me hard and said, "I'll be praying for you."

The next Friday, just before lunch, I was called into the boss's office and told that there was to be a massive layoff in the company, and I was one of them. This was very upsetting because I was the sole support of my three children. I decided to go to the Bible study since it was about to start. I told them that I had just been laid off. Carolyn said, "I'm so sorry. God told me that was going to happen last week. That was why I walked you to your office and said I'd be praying for you." That gave me much comfort because I knew that God knows the future and would be taking care of me.

Discussion

Sometimes God comforts us through others. Tell of a time that happened to you.

CHAPTER 21

91st Psalm

I turned my ex-husband over to support enforcement to try to get child support from him. He retaliated by suing me for custody of our children. They were twelve and thirteen years old and of age to pick which parent they wanted to live with. He had them convinced that the schools were easier in his town. He said they could swim at the neighbor's house and that he would buy them a three-wheeler if they would come to live with him. They were sold on the idea.

I was in a meeting at church. My heart was crying out, "God, I can't bear to lose my children. They will go into the woods and get bitten by a snake, and no one will go looking for them. They will not go to church and grow up not knowing You. I need something to hang on to." The leader of the class stopped and said, "I have a feeling that there's a word from God coming." We waited for what seemed like a long time but no word. The leader said, "I can't go on. I still feel like there's a word coming." Then a lady stood up and said, "Well, it's not exactly a word, but I feel compelled to read the 91st Psalm." I knew in my heart that my answer was coming. She started to read it. It was about God's love and protection. One part talked about stepping on an adder(snake), and it will not harm you. And it ended by saying that God would show us His salvation. I felt so much comfort. I was glad it was not a word but a scripture that I could read over and over again when I needed comfort.

Later we were in court. They called us into the courtroom. My ex had his lawyers and friends as character witnesses at his table. I sat alone as my lawyer was still finishing up with his previous case. The judge was not in yet. My heart was racing with fear. I looked up and saw letters above the court. It said, "In God We Trust." I thought this court is ruled by a higher court. I started praying as hard as I could. The judge came in and said, "I want to see the lawyers in my chambers." Later I heard what was said. The judge said that he was not going to put the children on the stand and make them have to pick which parent. He had already made up his mind. The children would go with their father for the summer and with their mother for the school year.

> Whoever dwells in the shelter of the Most High will rest in the shadow of the Almighty. I will say of the LORD, "He is my refuge and my fortress, my God, in whom I trust."
> Surely he will save you from the fowler's snare and from the deadly pestilence. He will cover you with his feathers, and under his wings you will find refuge; his faithfulness will be your shield and rampart. You will not fear the terror of night, nor the arrow that flies by day, nor the pestilence that stalks in the darkness, nor the plague that destroys at midday. A thousand may fall at your side ten thousand at your right hand, but it will not come near you. You will only observe with your eyes and see the punishment of the wicked.
> If you say, "The LORD is my refuge," and you make the Most High your dwelling, no harm will overtake you, no disaster will come near your tent. For he will command his angels concerning you to guard you in all your ways; they will lift you up in their hands so that you will not strike your foot against a stone. You will tread on the

lion and the cobra; you will trample the great lion and the serpent.

"Because he loves me," says the LORD, "I will rescue him; I will protect him, for he acknowledges my name. He will call on me, and I will answer him; I will be with him in trouble, I will deliver him and honor him. With long life I will satisfy him and show him my salvation." (Psalm 91:1–16)

Discussion

If you are worried about yourself or another person, put their name in these scriptures.

CHAPTER 22

Keebler Healed

My first dog lived to be almost seventeen years old. It was very hard to lose him. A neighbor talked me into going and looking at breeders because they had a new batch of cute puppies. I said I didn't think I was ready yet, but I couldn't resist seeing the little puppies. When I got there, they had many cute six-week-old puppies. Then I spotted a larger dog that was four months old. His cage was in the back away from the others. The owner said, "No one wants him. He has a cherry eye."

She showed me his eye. It was red and looked like when you pull the lower lid down and was covering most of his eye. She said, "I'll sell him to you for half price. You could have surgery to correct his eye." I felt so sorry for him; he would get so excited each time I walked by his cage. I couldn't leave him there unloved. So I bought him. I was not sure about having surgery. It probably would be expensive, and I wondered if it would make his eye dry. I brought him home, and again I'd pray every day for him to be healed. A week later, I looked at him, and both eyes were perfect.

Discussion

Again, God cares about things that concern us, small things and animals included.

CHAPTER 23

Cancer Scare

I had been in the hospital twice that summer. I was having terrible stomach pain, and it was swelling eight inches beyond my pants waist. They couldn't find what was wrong with me. I was home feebly trying to clean the bathroom when the phone rang. It was the doctor. He told me that my CA-125 levels were high, and they had made me an appointment with the cancer doctor. I called my friend Theresa and told her what had happened and asked her to be praying for me. I went back to cleaning the bathroom, scrubbing, and crying. I wasn't ready to leave my children and my life.

When I walked back into the living room, Marilyn Hickey was on the TV. She was reading scripture about our life was in God's hands. I thought, *Oh, I forgot about God.* I ran and grabbed my Bible. Now what was that scripture? Was it Job 10:12 or Job 12:10? I read them both. Job 10:12 says, "Thou hast granted me life and favor, and thy visitation hath preserved my spirit." Job 12:10 says "In whose hand is the soul of every living thing, and the breath of all mankind." I knew that since they said basically the same thing that it was a message from God. I felt such peace. Later that week I was having lunch with Theresa, and she asked if I was okay. I said, "Why did you ask?" She said because you told me the doctor said you had cancer. I said, "Oh, I forgot." God had given me perfect peace about it. Later when I went to the doctor the tests showed that I didn't have cancer.

Discussion

Have you ever felt that you were in a bubble of love above the problems going on around you?

> And the **peace** of God, which transcends all **understanding**, will guard your hearts and your minds in Christ Jesus. (Philippians 4:7)

CHAPTER 24

Josh

My daughter loved Josh. He was a special dog, so loving, friendly, and so smart. She had begun training him to be a search-and-rescue dog. One day he went missing, and Suzette was so worried. We drove around looking for him day after day. We put out posters for the missing dog with a reward. A month had passed and nothing.

One day, I had gone to a movie and turned my phone off. But somehow, it rang. I saw it was from Suzette, and I knew it was an emergency. I ran out of the theater and answered it. Suzette was in distress. She had gotten a call that they found a dog matching her description in another county. But it had been shot and was dead. Suzette was driving to see if it was Josh. She said, "Please pray." I knew it would take a miracle for Suzette to not be angry and bitter if this was Josh. I left for Suzette's house and met up with her friends. We prayed and waited to hear from Suzette. Finally, Suzette came home crying, with her dead dog in the back of the truck. We gather around her and hugged her and prayed. She was very hurt, but not angry or bitter. God comforted her. But I still wonder how that call came through in the movie when the phone was turned off.

Discussion

God can even control electronic things if needed.

CHAPTER 25

Job—Ask for It

I had left a good job, to pursue a different vocation that didn't work out. I then took a job in the oil-and-gas field like I previously was in. The new job was okay, but I missed my original job. I wished that I had not left it. All my friends were there. But I knew I couldn't get it back because there were only two people in the accounting department, and they had both been there for many years. Nothing would open up there for a long time. As I was cleaning the kitchen and thinking about all this, I felt like I heard, "If you want the job, you have to ask for it specifically." Wow, that caught me by surprise. I thought, *Okay, God, if you want me to have that job, then I'm asking for it specifically.* A few days later I received a phone call offering me that job, and they would restore my seniority time, so I didn't have to work up to more vacation time.

Discussion

Don't assume you can't have something you want. God wants you to ask for it and see if it's something God wants you to have.

CHAPTER 26

Financial Blessing

I was nearing sixty years old, and I only paid a few years on a thirty-year mortgage. I had some medical expenses that had drained my savings. And I was wondering how I would be able to retire when the time came.

I hated my current job. I felt like my supervisor hated me. I looked for another job but couldn't find one that would pay enough. This was the summer of 2005. I prayed, "God, I just want to quit my job even if I have to take a severe pay cut." I felt like He was telling me to stay until mid-2006. I wanted to argue, "Couldn't I just stay until Christmas, get a bonus, and quit?" I still felt like He was telling me mid-2006. So I stayed.

In October, I crossed the date to be tenured in the job. This meant I got a share of the profits. In November, the company decided to test the market and put the company up for sale. They got an offer that was way more than they expected. They signed the sale papers in January with the agreement that we would work through April to help them migrate to their computer. My share of the profits was enough to pay cash for a nice house and put money in my retirement fund.

Discussion

Don't make decisions without asking God. Even if the answer isn't what you want to hear, it will turn out for your best.

> But my God shall supply all your needs according to his riches in glory by Christ Jesus. (Philippians 4:19 King James Version)

CHAPTER 27

Job at Home

As I was getting older, I felt it would be good if I could work out of my house. That way I could work past retirement and still handle the work. I thought about how to make this transition. Maybe I could take on work at night and grow the business until I felt I could quit my full-pay job with the insurance and benefits. That would be hard to get enough business to meet my expenses. But then my company sold, and I was laid off with a share of the profits. I knew this would be the very best time to start a business from my house.

I got my business cards made, and I planned to update my resume and start going down the phone book calling on companies. The day I picked up my business cards, I went to a church group dinner. We liked to meet each year and catch up with each other. We were going around the table telling the others what was going on in our lives. I told them that my company had just sold, and I was hoping to work out of my house. A friend said, "I know someone. Do you have any business cards?" She put them in touch with me, and I was hired to work part-time out of their home. I went to the doctor and ran into one of my previous bosses. I told him that I was looking for another part-time job to go with the one I already had. He told his son, and I was hired. I was on my way to working out of my home.

Discussion

> I will bless her with abundant **provision**s;
> her poor I will satisfy with food. (Psalm 132:15)

CHAPTER 28

New House and Job at Home

My son couldn't drive because he had poor vision. He was staying in his room all day. I needed to find a new house that was near stores, restaurants, and the movie theater. I had been casually looking for a long time, but nothing felt right. One night I prayed, "God, I'm tired of looking. Just put me where you want me." The next day, I put my price range on the computer to look for houses, like I had done many times before. A house across the street from where I was working came up. I was so excited because I didn't think there would be any houses in that neighborhood in my price range. I called a realtor and saw the house, and I knew it was the right one.

I told the realtor that I would clean my house for a few days so I could sell it and then put the sign in my yard. She said, "Okay, but that she would go ahead and list it on the computer." Someone wanted to look at my house even though I told them I had not decluttered it yet. By the time I was off work that evening, I had bought and sold both houses in less than twenty-four hours. My realtor said she had not seen that happen in the thirty years she had worked.

When my boss saw that I had bought the house across the street, she started thinking. They had never been able to go on trips because they couldn't leave the FedExes that came to their front door. They contained checks, and you can't hold FedExes like you can the mail. She said that now I was so close I could check their front door every hour while they were gone. So they got to see their children and grandchildren. They liked it so much that they decided to move to Georgia to be near their children. They put me on full-time and put the software on my computer. We send info back and forth by computer. And now I was working full time out of my home.

Discussion

All these blessings were great but most important is knowing that God is with you and loves you and that you are never alone, and He will always provide for you.

> May he give you the desire of your heart
> and make all your **plan**s succeed. (Psalm 20:4)

The next are possibly visions. They are more vivid than dreams or thoughts.

CHAPTER 29

Under the Cross

We were about to have Communion, and I was praising with my eyes closed. I saw a bleak horizon with miles of nothingness. It felt so hopeless. I said, **"Jesus, save me."** Suddenly I was standing under the cross; it was very high up. Jesus was on the cross, and His blood was running down on me. It was like a shower, cleansing me outside and inside until I was totally clean.

Then Jesus was standing beside me. He said, "Come with me." He took me to God. God was pacing and very excited to see me. When He turned and saw me, He threw open His arms wide. He held me in the warmest hug, and I could feel His love just filling me up.

CHAPTER 30

Redeemed

We were in church, and the music leader was teaching us a new song that goes, "There's a song in my heart that the angels cannot sing—redeemed, redeemed." I thought, *Why can't the angels sing redeemed, and what does* redeemed *actually mean?* Immediately my mind raced back to years ago.

We were moving into our new home, but they were not through building it. It was chaos. People were bringing in furniture, and then the men were moving furniture trying to find a short in the electrical system. I tried to empty a bucket of water in the sink, but the drain was not hooked up. I tried to throw the water out the back window and nearly through it on someone. When we finally were finishing, the last thing to do was to hook up the dining room light fixture. It had a chain that hooked to a cut glass orb, and then to the light fixture itself. But the cut glass orb was missing. You could not attach the fixture without the orb. We looked for it and finally found it with some old boxes in the burn pile. God said, "That's what redeemed is. You were thought to be worthless and thrown out. I looked and looked for you and found you near the fire. I cleaned you up and placed you near the light. Where you reflect the light all around."

Discussion

"I have swept away your offenses like a cloud, your sins like the morning mist. Return to me, for I have **redeemed** you." (Isaiah 44:22)

CHAPTER 31

Child in Throne Room

I was in church and wanted to sing the praise songs, but I was feeling so guilty and unworthy to come to God. I closed my eyes, and I saw a huge throne room. The floors were shiny marble. There were soldiers lined up with tall hats and at full attention, like the soldiers you see at Buckingham Palace. Way in the distance, there was a magnificent throne where God was sitting. I was so intimidated by it all. Then I heard the clicking of a little girl's patent leather shoes. She was running toward the thrown with her arms open wide shouting, "Daddy!" God threw his arms open wide and scooped her up. He set her on His knee and smiled so proudly. Then I heard God say, "This is how I see you. Come to me. I love you."

Discussion

Don't let guilt keep you from God. That's Satan's biggest trick. God always wants you to come to Him.

> If we **confess our sins**, he is faithful and just and will forgive us **our sins** and purify us from all unrighteousness. (1 John 1:9)

CHAPTER 32

Crown

When we have praise songs at church, I like to close my eyes and feel God. One time, I felt like someone tall was standing very close in front of me. I peeped my eye open, but I didn't see anyone, but the feeling stayed. I knew it was Jesus standing there. With my eyes closed, I started to see a beam of light shining down. It looked like it was glowing dust particles except these were made of gold. Through the mist, I noticed reflections of brightly colored stones. As I peered to see more, a crown came into focus. Then Jesus said, "So you like my crown… Well, this one is for you." He lifted it off His head and was bring it down to my head. As I looked at the stones, I recognized that one was for loving my children, one was for being a friend, etc. I thought, *These are not things I did. They are blessings that were given to me.* I fell on my knees, and I understood why the four and twenty elders were casting their crowns at Jesus's feet.

Discussion

God isn't looking at just church attendance or tithing or outward things. He is looking at us as loving Him and loving people. God gives us the gift of love.

> The twenty-four elders throw themselves to
> the ground before the one who sits on the throne

and worship the one who lives forever and ever, and they offer their crowns before his throne, saying:

"You are worthy, our Lord and God, to receive glory and honor and power, since you created all things, and because of your will, they existed and were created!" (Revelation 4:10–11)

CHAPTER 33

Horse and Rider

I was in church, and the choir was singing the song "Alpha and Omega." It was about one of my favorite verses where New Jerusalem comes down, and God will dwell with His people and wipe away every tear. I had my eyes closed, and I kept seeing the aisle beside me. I tried to erase it, but it kept coming back. I thought, *Why would I see the aisle? I should at least see the front of the church.* Then I thought, *Why is there sunlight streaming in from the back? The back door was far away, and then the foyer; and also it was night.* Then I heard the sound of horse hooves in the distance. They were coming fast, and the sound got louder and louder. I could feel the pounding in my chest.

Suddenly, I saw a white horse with a rider. The rider wore all white, and His face was shining so bright that it was like looking at the sun. His thigh was a bronze color and muscular. On it was chiseled words, "King of Kings." He was followed by many horses and riders wearing white. They were rushing. The horse's necks were stretched out and their manes flying back and nostrils flared. The riders were leaning forward as in a race. They were packed close together, and there were so many, and the line streamed back into the distance until they became dots. They continued to rush by, and my heart raced the whole time. Then the top of the church was gone, and the horses rose and made an arch over a cloud and disappeared. I thought, *If this is Jesus, and He is followed by all the saints of the ages, then, where am I in all this?* At that moment, I felt like a huge magnet was in my chest drawing me up and into the arch.

Discussion

This may not be the way the rapture actually happens, but God gave me this vision to comfort me during a hard time.

The next are fictional stories that came to my mind to explain God and His kingdom.

CHAPTER 34

Lost Chick

It was starting to get dark, and a light mist of rain was starting. The little chick was lost. He ran cheeping this way and that but didn't know where to go. He was shivering with cold and fear. He was so tired, but if he'd fall asleep, he will be eaten by predators. There seemed to be no hope. Then he heard his mother calling for him. He ran toward the sound. He nestled next to her so close that he could feel the warmth of her body and hear her heartbeat. He was surrounded by his brothers and sisters, and his mother's feathers sheltered him. He could finally sleep because he knew his mother will protect him. He was so happy. That's how it is to come to Jesus.

Discussion

> He that dwelleth in the secret place of the most High shall abide under the shadow of the Almighty. (Psalm 91:1)

> He will shelter you with his wings; you will find safety under his wings. His faithfulness is like a shield or a protective wall. (Psalm 91:4)

CHAPTER 35

Adopted

There were two children in an orphanage. A loving couple came to visit and saw the first child. They asked if he would like to be their child, and he said no. Then the couple saw the second child. They asked if he would like to be their child, and he said yes. Later, the two children were talking at school. The first child asked, "What's it like being in that family? Do they boss you around and tell you what to do?" The second child said, "Yes, sometimes. They tell me to make my bed and clean my room. If I do it, then sometimes, we go out for ice cream. But they also give me a warm bed and my own bedroom and a bike. They make me feel safe and loved." So the second child decided to make his bed and clean up his stuff. But no one took him out for ice cream or did anything for him. He said, "I don't understand why I didn't get the ice cream and stuff. I did the same work." The first child said, "It's not because of the work I did. It's because I'm their child." It's the same way in God's family, and the offer to be His child is still open.

Discussion

Some people think by being good, they can earn their way to heaven. You must accept Jesus as your Lord and Savior to get the benefits of his kingdom (family).

> For you did not receive the spirit of slavery leading again to fear, but you received the Spirit of adoption, by whom we cry, "*Abba*, Father." (Romans 8:15)

Abba is like *Daddy*.

CHAPTER 36

Jail

There was a man on death row. He was begging everyone to save him. He told the jailer, "I promise to never hurt anyone again, and I'm a doctor, and I will spend my life helping others." The jailer said, "I wish I could let you go, but if I let you go, then others will not respect the legal system, and crime will run rampant in our country. You must pay your debt to society." Then the man said, "I found a fellow prisoner that is willing to pay my debt for me." The jailer said, "He will be paying his own debt to society so he cannot pay yours too."

Weeks passed and one day the Judge came and said "You are all free to go. We found a man that had not committed a crime and was willing to pay your debt. He was electrocuted today." All the prisoners cheered and jumped around then they ran out of the jail.

However, one man sat in the corner. The Judge asked, "Why aren't you going? You are free to go." The man said, "I've done too many horrible things. This man could not have paid enough to free me." The Judge said, "Don't underestimate the price that was paid for you. You see the man that paid the price was my Son."

Discussion

Jesus is the only way to be saved.

Don't think you are too bad to be saved. Jesus's power to forgive is greater than any sin.

> For this is the way God loved the world: He gave his one and only Son, so that everyone who believes in him will not perish but have eternal life. (John 3:16)

CHAPTER 37

Defective Human

An alien came to our planet and saw a baby. He said, "This human is defective. He had no hair and no teeth. He can't walk or talk. He is good for nothing." The man said, "He is not defective. He's my son, made in my image. I see all the things he will grow to do and be. He is very precious to me." Sometimes we see ourselves or others as the alien did, but remember, God sees us as this father does.

Discussion

We are made in the image of God. He loves us, and we are important.

> So God created mankind in his own image, in the image of God he created them; male and female he created them. (Genesis 1:27)

> **I can do all** this **through** him **who** gives **me** strength. (Philippians 4:13)

CHAPTER 38

Birth-Death

The little baby in the womb was very comfortable. Warm and well-fed, just rocking along in peace. Then it started to feel cramped. Then one day it felt like the walls were caving in on him, and there was pressure, and his head was hurting. *Why is this happening to me?* he thought. Suddenly, he burst forth into a bright light, and there were people around that loved him. They had been preparing a place for him to live and had great plans for him.

The child grew and went through many stages. He became a man and had many experiences. He was very comfortable with his life. He had had a career, marriage, children, and grandchildren, and life was good. Then he began to have an ache here and a pain there. Suddenly, it was getting very hard for him to breathe, and he was so tired. He thought, *Why is this happening to me?* Then he burst forth into an even brighter world. People who loved him were standing around. They had been preparing a place for him and had many wonderful plans for him.

Discussion

> My Father's house has many rooms; **if** that were not so, would **I** have **to**ld you that **I am go**ing there **to prepare a place** for you? (John 14:2)

CONCLUSION

If I haven't been clear on how to have a relationship with God, I will summarize it as best I can. In the beginning, God wanted someone to love. He created this beautiful world with you in mind. Then He created man. He said, "It is very good." He meant that it was perfect. There was no sickness, no death, and no fear; everything was perfect. God would come down and commune with man each day.

God said, "You can eat of every tree except the tree of knowledge of good and evil. If you do, you will surely die."

But we have an enemy, the devil. He came into the garden and started to plant seeds of doubt in man's mind. "Did God tell the truth? Wouldn't you like to be God and know good and evil?" Man decided that he would not trust God and turned his back on God and ate of the tree of good and evil. Ever since that time, man has been imperfect—greedy, selfish, and sinful. The only way to fix the world was for a perfect man to die in place of all mankind. But no man on earth was perfect. So God sent His own son, Jesus, to be that perfect man and die in our place. When He died on the cross, the curse was broken. Anyone who believes in and trusts Jesus will be made perfect in the coming new world, and we will have peace with God from now on.

To prove that this is true and that He has all power, after being dead for three days, Jesus rose from the dead.

ABOUT THE AUTHOR

Jean is a woman who found herself starting over in life with three children and no career. God helped her through all the challenges she encountered. She has had a full life, her three children are grown, and she enjoys a career in accounting. She likes to line dance, crochet, and go camping. Her experiences have given her a deep faith in God and peace.

Printed in the USA
CPSIA information can be obtained
at www.ICGtesting.com
LVHW052118141023
761015LV00072B/1102